THE WINDOW
A Reflection of Hope

THE *Window*

A REFLECTION OF HOPE

Olga J. Walker

Guardian BOOKS

Belleville, Ontario, Canada

THE WINDOW
A Reflection of Hope
Copyright © 2002, Olga J. Walker

All Rights Reserved. No part of this publication may be reproduced, stored in a retrieval system or transmitted in any form or by any means—electronic, mechanical, photocopy, recording or any other—except for brief quotations in printed reviews, without the prior permission of the author.

All Scripture quotations, unless otherwise specified, are from *The Holy Bible, King James Version*. Copyright © 1977, 1984, Thomas Nelson Inc., Publishers.

Scripture quotations marked NIV are from *The Holy Bible, New International Version*. Copyright © 1973, 1978, 1984 International Bible Society. Used by permission of Zondervan Publishing House. All rights reserved.

ISBN: 1-55306-413-5

For more information, please contact:

Olga J. Walker
AT:
www.emeraldhillbooks.com

Cover design by Sheila Bernal

Guardian Books is an imprint of *Essence Publishing*, a Christian Book Publisher dedicated to furthering the work of Christ through the written word. For more information, contact:
44 Moira Street West, Belleville, Ontario, Canada K8P 1S3
Phone: 1-800-238-6376 • Fax: (613) 962-3055
E-mail: info@essencegroup.com • Internet: www.essencegroup.com

Printed in Canada
by
Guardian BOOKS

*This book is dedicated to my husband, Donald L. Walker.
Your love, support and jubilant spirit
have hoveled my heart with warmth and laughter.
Thank you for not letting me give up on myself.*

*To my wonderful sons,
Jaylen Finley Walker and Jordan Alexander Walker.
You are the stars that bring
an abundance of light to my life.*

*To all the children and their families, whose lives have been,
are and are going to be touched by UIC—
The University of Illinois at Chicago Division of
Specialized Care for Children (DSCC).*

*With the purchase of this book,
10% will be donated to Friends of DSCC.*

table of contents

Acknowledgements................................9
Introduction...................................13

Part 1: Reflection of Hope

    Spare Me.....................................17
    Your Presence................................21

Part 2: Reflection of Hope (Dreams)

    Patience.....................................25
    Future Unknown...............................27
    Courage......................................30
    Pain...34
    Things Missed................................36

Part 3: Reflection of Hope (Dreams)

    Still Hope...................................41

Part 4: Reflection of Hope (Dreams)

Miracle 47
Life 51
The Day 55
This Battle Is Not Yours 57

Part 5: Reflection of Hope (Dreams)

Silent Emotions of Love 63
Stand 65
Never Alone 68

Part 6: Reflection of Hope (Dreams)

Mercy and Grace 73
Pathway Angels 75

Part 7: Reflection of Hope

The Window 79
The Beginning 83

"Oh Spirit" (Poem) 89
Book Reviews 91

acknowledgements

Special thanks to Aleen Hardin: In the beginning of our friendship you were watching me and you said that you learned so many things from my life, but what you didn't know is when I became ill I began to watch you and pull strength from the person that you had become. Your continuous encouragement for me was to one day share my story with others. Well "A," against all odds, with God's help, I did it! And on the completion of my first book, I extend a special thanks to you.

To my gracious parents, Tobia R. Hill and Clinton Hill, Jr. So often when I visit my window of hope the reflection is of the both of you—your unyielding love, your strength in life's battles, your response to the needs of others and your spirit of prayer have aided me on my journey. I thank God for you both and I thank you for always being there for me.

To my siblings—Juanita Hill-Pryor, Glynne Hill, Kimberly Hobson, sister-in-laws Vicki Hill, Elizabeth Walker and brother-in-law Paul Hobson—thank you for joining me in my fight. Even though we live miles apart, to hear your voices filled with words of love and encouragement have been a lasting melody to my heart.

*

To the many people and organizations that have flourished my family with a reflection of hope and assistance in the midst of our journey, thank you: The American Red Cross; University of Illinois at Chicago - Division of Specialized Care for Children - Peoria Regional Office; Chris Campbell R.N. B.S.N. Nursing Consultant; Dr. Shah; Dr. Geiss; Dr. Plunkett; Dr. Savings; Dr. Woerner; Dr. Gibson; University of Chicago Hospital staff; Children's Hospital of Illinois at OSF Saint Francis Medical Center; St. Francis Hospital and staff; Proctor Hospital and staff; Dr. Hernandez; Peoria, IL. Dr. Ash; Dr. Shappley; Dr. Shull; Dr. Sullivan; Dr. Moore; emergency staff at Methodist Hospital - Germantown and Baptist East Hospital; Dr. Reed; Dr. Byrd; Dr. Douglas; Memphis, TN Baptist Rehabilitation Hospital staff - Germantown, TN, and family friend Dr. Ray Matthews. Grace Calvary U.M.C.; St. Mark U.M.C., Chicago, IL; Bethel U.M.C.; Allen Enterprises; Mt. Zion Baptist Church, Peoria, IL; and my church family, Living Water Church, Memphis, TN.

*

To those who have been instrumental in helping me bring this book to fruition—thank you for keeping my vision before me. Your support and many hours of assistance have been a blessing: Sheila Bernal; Lisa Carter; Kristie Denman; Essence Publishing (Guardian Books); Aleen Hardin; Kimberly Hobson; Karla Randle-Jackson; Connie Jones; Dr. Reginald Martin; Rev.

A Reflection of Hope

Myron McCoy; Valesa Moore; Pastor Reginald Spight; Paula Spight; Donald Walker; Juanita Hill-Pryor; Barbara Wright-Pryor; and Creation Gallery's portraits; Pedro Angel, Living Water Church and sponsors.

Sponsors: Donald Walker; Clinton and Tobia Hill Jr.; Dereanzy Hicks, Juanita Hill-Pryor, Glynne and Vicki Hill; Paul and Kimberly Hobson, Elizabeth Walker, Arthur Walker, Joseph and Constance Walker, Sr.; Annie Walker, H.T. and Ida Lockard; Marie Walker; Robert and Addie Rogers; Marlon and Kristie Denman; Oliver and Gardenia Hicks; Alfred and Michelle Saulsberry; Robert and Julia Babbs; Andre and Sonia Holliday; Magnolia Moore; Tamika Moore; Valesa Moore; Anthony Moore; Sam and Janice Johnson; Frank and Jenice Upshaw; Anthony and Demetrius Evora; Roland and Deloris McJunkins; Tommy and Christine Davis; Jimmy and Mary Pollard; Michael and Karla Jackson; L.A. and Linda Randle; Vinnie and Geni Randle; Derrick and Connie Jones; Reginald and Paula Spight; Aleen Hardin; Beatrice and Salenia Williams; Toy and Aquilla Spight; John and Ann Springheart; Percy and LaVerne Green; Fannie Greer; James and Jean Miller; Vergia Hudson; Darren and Patricia McCoy; Michael and Carlotta Williams; Arnold and Debra Campbell; Darryl and Pariss Smith; Dr. Ray Matthews; James and Mattie Singletary; Vay Bogan; Sharon Colyer; George and Armentra Hicks; James and Samara Byrd; Mae Fitzgerald; Euzelia Vaughn; William and LaVerne Walker; Cora Hicks; Connie Hicks; Michael and Iris Fisher; Stacey McJunkins-Thompson.

In Loving Memory

Harry Leonard Pryor, III
Kisla B. Rogers
Ernest Walker
Tollie Bogan
Robert Vaughn
James H. Hobson
Charlene E. Hobson
Sylvia Williams
Lizzie Lobdell

To the other beautiful reflections in my life, thank you for your many prayers.

Introduction

This book will bring forth a clear reflection of how God's grace is sufficient and how His strength is made perfect in weakness (2 Cor. 12:9). Many tend to think that they are in control of their own lives, but without God's love, mercy and grace, we could do nothing. With God our lives can be a reflection of hope to many looking on. Sometimes in our lives we choose our own path to follow, but it is not always the path God has for us. At times God will bring us to a low point in order to use us more fruitfully toward His ends.

If one were able to see his or her life before it actually happened, would one try to change things or are the episodes of life unchangeable? Could one live and learn from life as it is? I guess that's something to think about. Most, I'm sure, would try to change many things… or maybe not.

As you look into this world of a young lady's life, in which chronic pain and disease entered her body at the blossoming age of twenty-six, you will find that she was totally unaware of the years to come—but the years of turmoil did come. Her life became unusual, not in a sense that thousands of women haven't experienced or are not experiencing the same, but it was unusual from the life she had envisioned for herself. She thought she had control over her life. She did not. Through all the physical pain she learned to depend on God's Word for her comfort and understanding. The scoops and dips of a roller coaster will gently describe the trials she faced.

As you read on, let the many words serve as a testimony and let the quotes from God's Word penetrate your soul. There will be sadness, disappointments, fear, loneliness, anger, but oh, there will also be times of joy, happiness and laughter. Over time there will be peace.

If you would please, clear your mind, search your heart and take not one thing for granted. Acknowledge how blessed you are.

PART ONE

Reflection of Hope

*Trust in the L*ORD *with all thine heart;
and lean not unto thine own understanding.
In all thy way acknowledge him,
and he shall direct thy paths.*

PROVERBS 3:5-6

spare me

The year had come. You know the year that you and your girlfriends have been planning for years? Yes, the girls' getaway, the vacation of all vacations. Three of my girlfriends and I—all from different walks of life, yet so much alike—decided to get away from the stresses of our jobs and our everyday lives and kick back and relax a little. The sad thing about it was that success had given each of us a vision of more success, not making us stop to think of the accomplishments at hand. This is not to say success isn't good, but what we lacked was the acknowledgement of where it all came from.

Well, at the last minute, my girlfriends had to cancel out. But this vacation for me (Noel) was much needed, so I went on the trip alone—or so I thought.

There she was, walking the Carolina Beach. The month was May and a warm breeze swept across the waters. She was draped in soft white gauze, pants rolled above her ankles, a long jacket flowing with the motions of her body, strap sandals

The Window

loosely hung from the pointer and index finger of her right hand and dark shades covering the mystery behind her brown eyes. With each gentle footstep her presence was known. Although surrounded by many, she often felt alone.

As Noel continued to walk in deep thought, her attention was drawn to a beautiful white church. The church was surrounded by crystal-like sand and adorned with beautiful glass windows. Noel stood admiring the beautiful sight as the church bells began to ring loudly from the highest steeple, sending the birds that rested there soaring over the waters. As the sun began to set at half-past six, the church doors opened and many people gathered outside. All seemed to be in good spirits, laughing and talking as they walked to their cars. Noel began walking slowly toward the glass window, and the closer she got to the window the faster her pace became as if there was an urgency to get there. The window looked as if it had been shattered and carefully glued back together, and, with all of its detail, it must have taken someone with a steady hand and much patience.

Noel carefully placed her hands on the sides of the window ledge as her sandals fell from her fingers into the sand. Out of curiosity, she looked inside. There she saw a young lady at the altar with her head hung low and her arms and hands stretched high. Noel focused on the young lady at the altar and noticed that she also was dressed in white gauze and was also barefoot. Noel noticed, from the side of the woman's face, tears that dropped from her eyes to the floor. The lady at the altar began to cry out, "Here I am Lord, a young, independent woman, self-sufficient, strong-willed, determined and excited about life. I come to you in hope that you will keep me on the path you would have me follow."

A Reflection of Hope

> *It's something how we can go to our Lord as if He doesn't know us.*

As she continued her conversation with God, Noel found herself weeping and her tears had become in sync with the lady at the altar. There was definitely a connection of souls in pain. Noel moved away from the window to go to her. As she stood and stepped away from the window, she heard a voice saying, "God will comfort her, you just be still." Noel took heed to that inner voice and pressed her face against the beautiful glass window and continued to look inside. The church was no longer a church on the inside. The walls were all white; there was no altar and the young lady inside was no longer there. Noel fell to her knees. Her thoughts were troubled not knowing exactly what it was that she was supposed to see or why exactly she was led to this particular window.

Noel raised her head and continued to look inside. There she lay. The lady who was at the altar was now on an operating table! The room was very sterile and still. She lay on the table surrounded by white walls. Her head was turned to one side and a white sheet covered her body from her feet to midway up her chest. Her body shivered from the cold air that blew through the room. From the way she lay on the operating table, very focused and humble, she seemed to have no fear, but surely she was afraid.

> *Sometimes we cannot see the pain and fear of someone by the way they look on the outside. Thank God for His son Jesus; He knows the heart.*

The Window

Suddenly she began to pray aloud: "Lord, God, don't let this slow me down because I'm still in search of that road that will lead me into the rest of my life. Guide the hands of the surgeons and I'll talk with You when You awake me." Once again she spoke as if God didn't know her concerns and fears. She did not know that God was the road that would lead her into the rest of her life.

The surgical team entered the room all suited up in their blue attire—little caps that covered most of their head and masks that covered their noses and mouths, leaving only their eyes showing. There was much conversation going on in preparation for the surgery as the nurse began to inject the anesthesia into her IV.

The lady's eyes closed and an oxygen mask was placed over her mouth and nose. She began drifting off in minutes, but just before she was totally unconscious, she opened her eyes and began to smile. It was if she heard a voice from heaven whispering in her ear, "I am with you now and I will always be with you. I'll be with you at that road that leads you into the rest of your life. The road is here and the beginning is now."

A cyst the size of a grapefruit was then removed from her right ovary.

Isn't it wonderful to have consolation in God?

your presence

Suddenly, after the operation, the lights inside the church went out. It was pitch dark on the inside and night had come upon Noel. She had been looking inside for many hours. Noel turned around and the moon and stars lit the beach. She picked up her sunglasses and sandals from the sand and began walking away from the church. Noel couldn't believe what she had seen; she turned around and ran back to the front doors of the church, hoping that the doors would be open. Her mind was on overload with questions as to who the lady inside the window was since her face had not been revealed. Noel shook the doors but they were locked. Then she called out, hoping someone would come and open the doors, but no one came.

Noel walked away thinking, "What a getaway this is turning out to be," pushing her feet through the sand as she headed to the beach house about a half mile up the beach where she was staying.

When she reached the four-room beach house she opened the door, turned on the light, dropped her sandals on the hall mat, placed her sunglasses on the hall table and headed toward the bedroom. When she reached the bedroom she flicked on the lights and began lighting the many candles that surrounded the room. She then prepared for a shower. While she was pulling her robe out of her bag, it felt as if someone was in her presence. Noel turned around in circles looking, but she couldn't see anyone.

She turned off the light and headed to the bathroom, her path lit by the flames from the candles. When her shower was completed, she put on her robe and fell across the bed exhausted from the evening. She lay on the bed quietly for a few minutes, and then she began to pray, something she never found time to do in her busy life. "Lord, thank you for this day even though at the end of it I'm totally confused. What is it you would have me to do with what I have seen today in the beautiful glass window of the church on the beach? Please reveal it to me before my vacation is over."

Part Two

*And not only so, but we glory in tribulation also:
knowing that tribulation worketh patience; and patience,
experience; and experience, hope: and hope maketh not ashamed;
because the love of God is shed abroad in our hearts
by the Holy Ghost which is given unto us.*

Romans 5:3-5

patience

The next morning, the sun beaming through the bamboo shades woke Noel. She sat up in her bed and thought it was wonderful to wake up and not have to do anything. This vacation was much needed for Noel; she needed to clear her head of many things going on in her busy life.

After that thought, a light went off in Noel's head—the window… that beautifully designed window at the church on the beach! Noel jumped out of bed and dressed for the day. After she dressed, she went to the kitchen, grabbed a bagel, spread cream cheese on it, gobbled it down and headed out the door. She was so anxious to get to the glass window to see if she would see anything that day.

Noel ran a half a mile up the beach to the church. All of the activities going on around her were blocked out; she couldn't hear or see the people around her. Noel's only focus was to see what was beyond the window. She once again rested on her knees as she looked over the bottom ledge into the window. She saw the sanctuary lit up with a rainbow draping from two

The Window

colorful stained glass windows on each side of the sanctuary, and the lady was not there. When Noel stood up to walk away, she heard a voice saying, "Don't look for me here, I will come to you in your dreams."

> *I guess everyone, at some point in his or her life, will wonder, "Why am I here?"*

"What is my purpose and what am I supposed to be doing? Why is it that I stand here at the top of a ski slope with no skis and a gust of wind slowly approaching? Will I be swept away down the slope in fear of losing my life before I find out my purpose? Or will my faith keep me from falling?"

> *God wants us to make choices in life and, when that unexpected gust of wind comes and sweeps you off your feet and down a ski slope with no skis, I hope you will have already chosen God.*

future unknown

The day had passed and night had come, with Noel still wondering about the window as she cuddled up with a good book. While reading, Noel fell asleep and began to dream.

"Hello Noel, it's me."
"Me who?" said Noel.
"Me, the lady in the window."
"Why can't I see you?"
"It's not for you to see me yet, just listen...."

I tried for three years to conceive a child; my body and spirit grew tired. I had undergone a major surgery after marrying my husband who spoke of having children after two weeks of courtship. The conversation at the time was just that—conversation—and taken very lightly.

After I said "I do," I became sick two days into our honeymoon cruise. I began to hemorrhage, not from a ruptured blood vessel, but from an early cycle. The pain grabbed me and doubled me over. I thought I had timed everything perfectly, but oh, was I surprised.

Lying in a fetal position, not saying much and feeling bad, I sent my groom off to enjoy the rest of the evening. A couple of hours went by and tears began to roll from my eyes as I gazed into the darkness from the cabin window, wondering to myself, "What is this excruciating pain that has come upon me in the beginning of my new journey, in the midst of feeling as if I were a princess in my husband's eyes, headed toward a bright future?"

My prayer that night had become a plea to relieve me from the pain and bleeding with which I was not familiar. While I gobbled down extra-strength Tylenol, my husband returned, showering me with gifts. Now that's something that could make a girl's pain subside for a moment! I thanked him with a gentle kiss, apologizing for Mother Nature's extraordinary work.

The next morning the pain and bleeding subsided enough for me to enjoy the rest of my honeymoon cruise. My prayer/plea had been answered. After such a drastic change in the pain and bleeding from the previous night, I just chalked it up to stress from the prenuptial planning and the excitement from the wedding. I had no way of knowing, at the time, that this was the beginning of a series of problems that would impact many years to come.

A Reflection of Hope

*Life has its way of throwing you for a loop.
When you least expect it, in a blink of an eye,
your life could change.*

*Isaiah 41:10—Fear thou not; for I am with thee:
be not dismayed; for I am thy God: I will strengthen
thee… yea, I will uphold thee with the right hand
of my righteousness.*

courage

Hello Noel, it's me.

After returning from my honeymoon, I was feeling fine until a month later when it was time for my cycle to start. The pain and bleeding this time were worse than before. I visited several gynecologists that month in hopes they would be able to tell me what was going on, but each visit was a dead end. I had been told I had a stomach virus; I was told I might be pregnant and it was too early to tell; I was told that maybe I could try birth control pills to regulate my cycle, but nobody could justify the pain along with the severe bleeding. Nothing was concrete, and no test had been done. I became frustrated and scared.

I shared my concerns with a friend, and she referred me to her gynecologist. I finally called my friend's gynecologist, and I was able to get an appointment the next day. I hardly slept, tossing and turning with worry. The next day I went for my appointment. I sat in the office nervously filling out medical forms, my hands quivering as I wrote and I thought I would never finish, but as soon as I did, the nurse called me into the examining room. I spoke with her for a few minutes, she took my vitals and soon the doctor knocked and entered the room. She appeared to be very nice. The doctor sat in a chair, began to ask the regular routine questions and then I told her my symptoms. She examined me and she said, "Everything seems to be okay, but to be sure, I want some other tests to be done." She left the room and told the nurse to schedule a sonogram that day. When I came out of the examining room, I was sent to the hospital for my test.

When I made it over to the hospital, I registered and sat down in the waiting room until my name was called. I picked up several magazines and began flipping through the pages one by one, not really reading any of them. I was really nervous.

After about thirty minutes my name was called, and I jumped up out of my seat and the magazines in my lap fell to the floor. I slowly reached down to pick them up as the other patients watched. The nurse took me to the changing room and told me to remove all of my clothes, put them in a locker and put the gown on with the opening in the front. I said "okay" and she closed the door saying, "When you're done step out and I'll take you for your sonogram." I had had a sonogram before, but that did not stop me from being a little on edge. When I stepped outside the room, I was escorted to a very dark room, all except the light from the equipment. I was told to lie on the table, a white sheet was then placed over me and folded down at my lower abdominal area. I was then told that with this sonogram, they should be able to see what was causing so much pain.

The technician turned the screen away from me, squeezed some cold gel onto my abdominal area and began pressing down and moving the sonogram probe all around. The two technicians began talking amongst themselves, and I began to ask them questions: "What do you see? Is it bad?" But it was if I wasn't being heard. They wouldn't answer me. Then one of the technicians left the room and came back with a doctor. He looked at the screen and patted my arm as if to say, "It's going to be okay." Then the doctor said, "Get dressed and we will get your gynecologist on the phone." At that point I was acting frantic. "What did you find?" But they were not at liberty to tell me.

Well I got dressed quickly and went to the office in which they had my doctor on the phone. The nurse told me to sit down, and she would be back in a few minutes. I nervously picked up the phone and said, "Doctor, what is it"? She said, "The sonogram shows that you have a dermoid tumor on the inside of your right ovary, and it has to be removed at once; this will also mean that half of your ovary will have to go. I will do a biopsy to determine if it is cancerous or not."

"Cancer?"

She said, "Yes."

I hung up the phone and was so upset from the news I couldn't pull myself together to drive home. I sat in the lobby for a few minutes, crying my heart out, then went to the pay phone and called my husband at work. He was out to lunch, so I called my girlfriend and she came and drove me home.

Surgery was done two days later. A forty-five minute surgery turned into three hours because they discovered I also had a severe case of endometriosis, an infertility disease. Thank God the tumor wasn't malignant. So one problem was laid to rest and another one was awakening.

Noel, please remember this: never lose hope, depend on God and God alone.

A Reflection of Hope

Psalm 31:24—Be of good courage, and he shall strengthen your heart, all ye that hope in the LORD.

pain

Hello Noel, it's me. I still have lots to tell you.

Early on, the endometriosis had become so painful and severe I couldn't stand on my own two feet. Many days I had to crawl to the kitchen and sit on a chair at the stove to prepare dinner. I went from having a career and doing it all to being totally dependent on my new husband for my well-being. At that time, he felt pain was manageable by my mental state—mind over matter: "If you think you have no pain, somehow it will go away or not be as bad." He once said to me, "I played football in pain every day, but I didn't quit," and just by that comment I felt as if he didn't understand. I imagine it brought on stress for him with all the responsibility suddenly sitting on his shoulders. I also felt afraid because I didn't know how this would affect our immature marriage. Although football was a choice for my husband, I was faced with a game of pain I had not chosen to play.

The unspoken emotions he must have felt.

The hopelessness he must have felt not being able to heal the pain of someone he loved.

A Reflection of Hope

The courage he must have had knowing that, from day to day, his words might not be enough to soothe the soul of someone he loved.

The strength he found to stay focused on the foundation he had built when the walls continued to fall around someone he loved.

The anger he must have felt within, not being able to prescribe the cure for someone he loved.

The faith he needed to encourage that someone he loved.

The joy that came knowing he was never alone and neither was the someone he loved.

The peace that seals God's love, knowing He has control over that someone He loves.

> *Psalm 33:22—Let thy mercy, O LORD, be upon us, according as we hope in thee.*

things missed

Hello, Noel it's me.

I often thought of the many things I excluded myself from because of one or a few of the ailments I faced. For my ten-year high school reunion, I had been married for two years and found myself living in a body in which I was not comfortable. I had been on a very potent medication prescribed for a severe case of endometriosis. It was bad enough knowing childbirth would be difficult for me, if it would happen at all. It was something how my mind would go haywire when I was told I may not be able to have something I had always yearned for. In order for me to function at the time, this drug was prescribed. My body had become crippled in pain from this infertility disease. It had become very difficult for me to even move around without crawling or bending over at the waist to get from point A to point B. There were days I would scream and rock for relief. Not only was the physical pain an issue, but, after about a month or two of taking my medication, my voice began to change, my hair fell out, I blew up like a balloon, menopause set in, and I suffered with short-term edema— swelling of the joints. Well, in October, my parents received a call from one of my high school classmates. I don't remember which one, but the call was to get in touch with me for my ten-year class reunion which would take place in the summer. When I received the message I instantly panicked because of the way I looked and felt at the time. I didn't know what made me so afraid. I guess the reactions I may have gotten from my classmates frightened me, but I didn't give them a chance. These were people with whom I'd shared four years of my life, learning, laughing, growing and experiencing the joys of being a high-school student. They were great years of my life. Oh how the years came and rolled away so quickly, sending everyone in many different directions. The night of the dance I sat alone in my room, imagining all the smiling faces I once knew.

Noel, it's okay to have emotions that no one else understands.

> *Joshua 1:9—Have I not command thee?*
> *Be strong and of a good courage; be not afraid,*
> *neither be thou dismayed: for the LORD thy God*
> *is with thee whithersoever thou goest.*

PART THREE

Reflection of Hope (Dreams)

*Blessed is the man that trusteth in the LORD,
and whose hope the LORD is.*

JEREMIAH 17:7

still hope

Hello, Noel it's me. There is still hope.

After trying some of everything to conceive a child, in vitro fertilization was one of the options which my husband and I decided to try. This was a stressful process. First of all, at this point we had been commuting to Chicago from Peoria for a year, and the travel was about 150 miles each way. I was seeing an endocrinologist who specialized in infertility. My husband and I were determined at this point because the travel had become costly and tiring, but we were committed to doing what we had to do to conceive a child. I had to take a series of shots—one a day for ten days—in hopes of stimulating my ovaries to produce mature eggs. If this procedure worked, my husband would have to travel back to Chicago so that we could complete the procedure.

Every day my sister gave me a shot in my hip, and I would go every day to the hospital to be monitored and to see, through a sonogram, if today would be the day I would call my husband. Well, after two days, there wasn't any good news. I called my husband every night to give him an update. After the fourth day I began to get worried, and that night when I called my husband I guess he could hear it in my voice. My husband said to me, "We will continue to pray and keep the faith."

On the fifth day my cousin came by my parents' house and sat with me with only words of encouragement. While we were sitting talking, the telephone rang. I was called to the phone at the end of the hall. To my surprise it was the hospital calling with bad news. I remember saying, "Is it time, should I call my husband?"

There was a silent pause, and then the nurse said, "I'm sorry, but the doctor has given orders to stop the shots because there are still no eggs and usually, after the third or fourth day, there should have been eggs produced. I'm sorry," the nurse said again, and asked if my husband and I could come in one day the following week to discuss more options.

At that point I dropped the phone and began to scream hysterically, crying, falling to my knees and hitting the floor with the palms of my hands. It was if I had just lost a loved one. My cousin and others in the house came running from every direction, down the hall, up the stairs, yelling, "What's wrong? What happened?" My older sister reached me first, asking, "What's wrong?" I couldn't answer her, but I remember pulling on her leg to just help me. At that point she noticed the phone off the hook. She picked up the receiver and said, "Who is this?" and I remember her asking, "So what does this mean?" Then she said, "Oh my God" and hung up the phone. Before I knew it she was on the floor with me, holding and rocking me in her arms, telling me, "It's going to be okay." My cousin moved closer with my mother right behind her. My sister got up and guided my mom to another room to tell her the news while my cousin helped me up and down the hall to my bed. I lay in bed for hours, exhausted in my thoughts and numb in my faith. My cousin sat and held my hand, I'm sure in a silent prayer. This day was the day that I actually felt empty inside. After being filled with such hope and dreams, I was sad beyond belief by the thought of calling my husband to awake him with the news. Later in the evening I made that call; my husband too was sad to receive the news, but he also said we could try again in ninety days. But I had made up in my mind that, physically and emotionally, I couldn't go through the process again. I was tired; my body and soul had just had enough. From his silence, I could tell my response was a surprise to my husband. He knew I was a fighter, but I could no longer fight. He said he would come in the morning to get me. The next morning he came and took me home.

Noel, the weakness that slipped into this journey had brought on a feeling which I never imagined. The pain I'm sure wasn't the worst pain, but it belonged to me. I wondered if I had disappointed God in my weakness, in my world in which I sat so lonely. I wondered if I had disappointed God in my fear, anger and lack of faith. I wondered if I had disappointed God when I couldn't cry out to him in the midst of my sorrow.

Psalm 116:1-6—*I love the* LORD, *because he hath heard my voice and my supplications. Because he hath inclined his ear unto me, therefore will I call upon him as long as I live. The sorrows of death compassed me, and the pains of hell gat hold upon me: I found trouble and sorrow. Then called I upon the name of the* LORD... *and righteous; yea, our God is merciful. The* LORD *preserveth the simple: I was brought low, and he helped me.*

Part Four

*Reflection of Hope
(Dreams)*

*And Jesus answering saith unto them, Have faith in God.
For verily I say unto you, That whosoever shall say unto this
mountain, Be thou removed, and be thou cast into the sea; and
shall not doubt in his heart, but shall believe that those things
which he saith shall come to pass; he shall have whatsoever he saith.
Therefore I say unto you, What things soever ye desire, when ye
pray, believe that ye receive them, and ye shall have them.*

Mark 11:22-24

miracle

Noel! Noel! Hello it's me.

After trying everything but swinging from a chandelier to get pregnant, it finally happened. After much medication, shots and disappointment, my husband and I decided to adopt. To celebrate, we went away to the Carolina beaches for a couple of weeks to relax. Four days into our vacation, after having a wonderful seafood dinner, I became very sick with headache, fatigue and nausea. I began to vomit non-stop.

After going through in vitro about a month previous, I just thought I was having late effects from the medication. I knew that I wasn't pregnant—my faith had become weak— but my husband's faith stood strong. After trying for three years and being told by many to give it up, I guess I had become used to negative results. Right after that crazy thought my husband said, "You think you might be pregnant?" I just smiled with no response. My husband grabbed the phone and began calling my doctor in Chicago. The lines stayed busy, so he called my sister in Chicago and told her my

THE WINDOW

symptoms and asked her to keep trying to call the doctor. In about thirty minutes, my sister called back and said the doctor wanted me to take a pregnancy test. My husband hung up the phone with a blank look on his face. He then came to the side of the bed where I was lying and said, "Are you up to taking another pregnancy test?" I told him it would only be the 200th test in three years, why not? My husband ran out the door, yelling as he ran, "I'll be right back!" I rolled and rolled in the bed until my husband returned, and, when he did, he helped me to the bathroom to take the test. When I finished the test, I sat it on the top of the sink and made it back to the bed. My husband stood beside the bed again and said, "Are you ready for the results?" I said, "Yes," and he said, "Mommy, we're going to have a baby." I jumped out of the bed, grabbed my husband in a tight embrace, thanked God over and over and over again, and then I fainted. When I came to, my husband was sitting on the bed beside me, having his moment with God I'm sure.

Wanting to share our great news, I grabbed the phone and began calling everyone we could think of. The excitement and joy in my husband's face was just as I'd seen it in my dreams. Even though, for three years, my husband and I were disappointed over and over, pregnancy test after pregnancy test, doctor visit after doctor visit, medication and more medication, God had showed up and revealed His awesome power, and my underlined faith was restored. The next day my condition worsened. I continued vomiting without even eating or drinking anything, so our vacation ended early. When we made it back home, I was hospitalized right away for dehydration. After being in the hospital for two days I was released, but after returning home I still couldn't keep anything down—crackers, Jell-O, not even water. The next day I was admitted into the hospital again; sonograms were done and the baby seemed to be doing fine. I was in the hospital for four weeks due to hyperemesis gravidarum, but, after the third week, my doctor thought it would be best to start a feeding tube so my baby could start getting the proper nutritional supplementation as well as for symptomatic treatment of nausea. A long spaghetti-like rubber tube went up my nose, down my throat, into my stomach cavity and a milk-like liquid slowly dripped into my stomach.

After the fourth week my insurance company decided I could go home with the feeding tube. The feeding machine rested on a tall stand with wheels and beeped every time the liquid ran out. Every morning about 2 a.m. my husband was bumping through the house, half asleep, to prepare my feeding. We were getting well prepared for our little one's a.m. feedings. This went on for four months.

Two days before Christmas we were scheduled to go to my parents' house in Chicago. I had been so ill and confined to the bed and house; you can only imagine how excited I was. I had been through seven feeding tubes in four months, and I just didn't want to drag all of the feeding equipment out of town, so, right before we left, I pulled the tube out and put my trust in God that He would take care of me and my baby on our trip. When we reached our destination I was so sick my husband and my father had to carry me to bed.

All the while, I kept praying and calling on Jesus for strength, and, sure enough, He delivered me. By the third day I was eating everything in sight. And, on June 10, 1994, my nine-pound fifteen-ounce son was born, and it made all of the suffering worth it.

The Window

Noel, as they laid him on my breast, I felt his curly hair beneath my chin. I was overwhelmed with joy that God had allowed me to partake in bringing forth a miracle.

> *Mark 9:23—Jesus said unto him, If thou canst believe, all things are possible to him that believeth.*

life

Hello Noel, it's me.

After six months, the doctors thought I should try to get pregnant because I had started having abdominal pains again. But after going through a C-section with my first child, I thought it was too early. My husband and I talked it over and decided to wait. When my son turned one year old, we prayed and began trying. In four months I was pregnant.

The first three months I experienced morning sickness, but, after the fifth month, I started to experience a lot of pain in my lower back and abdominal area. After checking it out my doctor found another cyst on my left ovary which was increasing in size as my baby grew. This made it very difficult to walk.

In my seventh month on my way to get a hamburger in knee-deep snow, I was in a car accident. A car came speeding out of an alley and hit me in the front driver's side. The police were called, and at the time I felt okay. My car was still driveable, so I went on to get my hamburger and drove home.

The Window

I ate my burger and laid down on my bed. Soon after, I started experiencing more pain than usually in my lower back and all over my stomach area. I drove myself to the hospital which was about three minutes from my house, and, when I got there, the hospital staff rushed me in and began examining me. Sure enough, I had gone into premature labor.

My husband was called, and he rushed to the hospital, praying all the way, he said. When he entered my room, I could see the fear in his eyes. He slowly walked to my bedside and held my hand, saying, "It's going to be okay." The doctor came in and told me they were going to give me medication to stop the contractions and that I would have to be admitted into the hospital for a couple of days for observation. When I was released from the hospital, the rest of my pregnancy was spent in bed. It was hard having a little one and my husband working, but, with help from friends and my parents coming on the weekends, I made it through.

On March 20, 1996, my second son was born at nine pounds, eleven ounces. My precious baby boy was born and my husband and I had been blessed. God had once again allowed me to partake in bringing forth another miracle. When the nurse brought my son to me, I had undergone a two-hour surgery having my tubes tied and being packed with a dissolving gauze called "intercede" to help prevent adhesions and scar tissue from badly reoccurring. I looked into my baby's eyes and felt that something was wrong. Something about his eyes wasn't right. His eyes looked very tired and dark. I questioned the doctor about his health, and they said he was perfectly fine. But, as a mother, I knew something was wrong. I pulled my mother close to me and shared my concerns, and she began looking him over, saying, "All we can do is pray."

A Reflection of Hope

In two days I took our baby home where his big brother was patiently waiting. Our days went on as normal with our new addition, but his three-week check-up was not normal. After my son was examined the doctor told me to have a seat, and, at that point, my heart dropped. He informed me that my son had a heart murmur, and he had to have an EKG (electrocardiogram) done to see exactly where the murmur was. We would have to start seeing a pediatric cardiologist to follow his condition.

After leaving the doctor's office I was devastated. I placed my baby in his car seat and began driving slowly out of the parking lot. I was blinded by my tears, so I began to pray, "Lord please get me to my destination safely." I was about fifteen minutes from my home, and I knew I couldn't make it that far. Before I knew it I was pulling into my girlfriend's driveway about five minutes from the doctor's office. Walking to her front door, I had just enough strength to carry my son while God carried me. I rang the doorbell, and my friend opened the door with a friendly, "what a big surprise!" I placed my son in her arms and made my way to an armchair that was right off the foyer. The arms on the chair held me upright as I instantly fell apart. My friend didn't know what was happening, holding the baby and trying to comfort me. I told her the news that I had just received from the doctor. She got on her knees, holding the baby in one arm and opening her other arm for me to rest my weary body. As I tried to control my tears, she began to tell me about a friend of hers and her baby that had the same problem and that baby was three years old and doing fine. That testimony brought a wonderful reflection of hope in the midst of my scattered emotions.

Two weeks later after having the EKG the doctors informed my husband and I that there was a large hole between the right and left lower ventricle (ventricular septal defect) which separates the two sides of the heart, making the heart work harder and allowing more blood to travel to the lungs and become congested. This type of heart defect usually mends itself by the time a child turns one.

Well, by the time our son turned one, the hole had began to close, but it was not closing properly. Four months later my son had dropped a whole percentile on the growth chart. He wouldn't eat, was drained of energy and he slept for much of the day. I remembered just holding him in my arms, stroking his brow and singing, "You are my sunshine" as my heart cried out for my son's life.

Noel, the same God that created man has the power to fix whatever is broken.

> *Genesis 2:7—And the LORD God formed man of the dust of the ground, and breathed into his nostrils the breath of life; and man became a living soul.*

the day

Hello, Noel it's me.

Well, now comes the day of my hysterectomy. I thought after this surgery I would be on my way back to a "healthy" life and lifestyle. I thought this was going to be the end of my medical problems. I dreamed of waking up in the middle of the night with no pain.

I had an enlarged uterus that couldn't be explained, yet it was keeping up a lot of problems. I had a biopsy done to see if cancer was the cause. Several other tests were done and nothing could be found. So this was my option, at thirty-two years old—to have a partial hysterectomy. At first I was devastated; I didn't want to be cut again. I thought of my children, and then I thought of all the wonderful things that would transpire after I had this done. I thought I would be as good as new. I thought I would be able to be that person I once was with no pain. But, sure enough, after surgery I was faced with something else.

It has been a true blessing to have known and experienced no pain and pain that brought me to the feet of Jesus when I couldn't fight the pain any longer. God had His way of making me acknowledge Him.

> *Psalm 62:5—My soul, wait thou only upon God; for my expectation is from him.*

this battle is not yours

Hello, Noel it's me.

When my son turned twenty months, my husband and I were informed that my baby boy had to have open-heart surgery. As my husband and I sat at the large round conference table with the cardiologist, going over the procedures and what we would have to prepare for, I became numb. The only feeling that I felt was my son's faint breath on my neck. The news had turned our lives upside down.

When it rains it pours; I also found out a week prior to this that I had to have a partial hysterectomy. My husband had recently started a new job and his insurance hadn't kicked in yet, and I had left my job to care for my son. My husband and I were faced with our worst nightmare. Where would we get the money to pay for the surgery for my son as well as the surgery that I had to have? As my son's health diminished and my pain increased, my husband struggled within himself to figure out what we could do. I became like a mad woman desperate to find assistance. If we sold everything we had and cashed in our life's savings, we still wouldn't have enough to pay for the office visits which was over $700 each visit, and we had to make a office visit every seven days, not to mention the expense of the heart surgery.

One day, as I poured my heart-felt concerns upon a friend, she told me to call the American Red Cross. They couldn't do anything, but they gave me a name of an organization that could possibly assist me: University of Illinois at Chicago, Division of Specialized Care for Children, Peoria Regional Office. When I called I didn't know that a blessing was at the other end. As I told the lady that answered the phone my situation, I began to cry and the spirit of hope within me cried out to Jesus to send a blessing for my son. Many questions were asked, followed by an application being mailed to my home for me to complete. In a couple of weeks I received a letter that informed us we were eligible for full assistance. Not only were we going to receive over $260,000 for the surgery, they also paid for the office visits and my son's medication.

Noel, there is nothing too difficult for God to work out. During the six weeks of my recovery, my husband and I started to prepare the boys for my youngest son's heart surgery. My oldest son was a trooper. He was three years old, and he kept our spirits up with his spunky personality and always offering help with the baby. We explained to our oldest son that Mommy and Daddy were going to be with his little brother at the hospital and that his auntie and cousin were coming to stay with him and put him on the school bus and be there to get him off the bus at the end of the day. Then my oldest son climbed onto my lap, took my face in his two little hands and asked, "Will you bring my brother back home to me?" At that point tears welled up in our eyes and I said, "Sure we will, as

A Reflection of Hope

soon as he feels better. God will take care of your baby brother." My baby knew that his heart was going to be fixed, and, at that age, that's about all he could understand.

The night before the surgery some of our friends called a prayer meeting at our home. We prayed over the baby and prayers went up for my husband, my oldest son and I. Tears moistened the carpet where we stood, and hugs of comfort went throughout the room. When I went to put the baby to bed my pastor's sister followed me into the room; as I laid the baby in his crib, she said, "How are you doing? You're holding up so well, I couldn't do it if it was me."

I told her, "What you see is not me, it's the work of the Lord." This was a boo-boo Mom and Dad couldn't kiss and make better, so we turned it over to Someone who could.

She took me in her arms and whispered in my ear, "You're right, this battle is not yours."

The day had come for our son's surgery. Precious as a lamb he was as they took him from my arms at the hospital. The feeling that came over me at that moment was overwhelming, and I couldn't hold back the tears that showered my fainting spirit. My husband and I felt so helpless and afraid, yet we knew God would be with him. While we waited many family members and friends took off work to come and be with us, offering us prayer and encouraging words of comfort. Noel, I have come to know that prayer changes things. After three hours of surgery our baby boy was taken up to the Pediatric Intensive Care unit where my husband and I were able to go see him. When the doctors pushed the doors open for us to enter, I became very weak and my husband had to keep me from falling. Tubes and machines were everywhere. It seemed unbelievable that all of the equipment could be hooked up to such a small body.

The Window

My husband and I stood over him as tears rolled down our faces, overjoyed with the success of the surgery. I reached out to touch my baby's forehead and he opened his eyes for only a few seconds, saw his mom and dad, then stuck his thumb in his mouth. My husband said, "He's going to be just fine." My family had once again been able to experience the work of the Lord.

> *2 Chronicles 20:17—Ye shall not need to fight in this battle: set yourselves, stand ye still, and see the salvation of the LORD with you.*

Part Five

*Reflection of Hope
(Dreams)*

*Be completely humble and gentle;
be patient, bearing with one another in love.
Make every effort to keep the unity of the Spirit
through the bond of peace.*

Ephesians 4:2-3 (NIV)

silent emotions of love

Hello, Noel it's me.

I had become very lonely in my world. I had been so wrapped up in fighting health issues that my marriage was hurting. After being sick and in and out of hospitals so often, the stress of it all was taking a toll on my marriage. I felt that my husband didn't understand what I was going through, and my husband felt as if I didn't care about the load on his shoulders, but what he didn't know is that a lot of my pain was for him. Over time medical bills and finances had become our worst enemy. Sacrifices for both had to be made. Even though many blessings had transpired in this time, I found myself waddling in guilt, feeling as if my ailments were bringing on many problems. I had begin to allow an outside force to influence my faith. I began to feel more than physical pain: my heart ached, my fears of being alone were hidden and my tears were dried before I could blink.

Trying not too disrupt the silent emotions of my husband, I saw him drifting away in worry. After many years my ailments had taken a toll on him, also. He slipped into a sad spirit, wanting so badly for his bride to be well.

My spirit had become weak, my heart broken, my ears rang with the sound of cruel voices around me. The walls of my home bled with tears. One day, when I couldn't bear it anymore, I fell on my knees and called on my Lord and Savior to help me in my despair. When I raised my head, there he was, my husband, standing at the door with open arms asking me to come. As I went to him words flowed from my heart: "I stretched forth my arms and my hands are filled with gratitude for all that you have encountered with me. The road has been narrow and many curves and detours have taken place. As we travel a road unknown I thank you for loving me in spite of all of my challenges. In so many ways your silent love had given me strength to go on. When I had nothing to give, I had love and I thank you for accepting that and loving me all the same."

God wanted to change my husband and I before He changed our circumstances.

Psalm 25:17—The troubles of my heart are enlarged: O bring thou me out of my distresses.

stand

Hello, Noel it's me.

Once again I walked away from a physician's office in shock and very disturbed by their findings. I walked from the examining room to my car. While walking I became weak, my limbs were like noodles and tears began to well up in my eyes. As I began to replay the conversation with the dermatologist in my mind, I heard her say, "You have alopecia," which is premature hair loss. I heard her, but at that moment it did not register with me.

The dermatologist and her assistant sat on the edge of their chairs looking as if they would need to catch me when they told me I would have to cut my hair off to remove the chemicals in my hair. But much to their surprise I sat up in my chair and began to pack up the many bottles of medication in my bag. I replied to the doctor, "Open up my file and, if you would closely review the information I have given you about my medical history, you'll understand my response to such devastating news," I said, with much confidence. "I have had many challenges in my life, more so over the past eight years, and yet with God I still stand."

The doctors then replied, "Did you hear me? You will have to cut your hair off."

I responded, "Did you hear me? With God I will stand. I'm sure it will be hard like many other challenges that have come before me, but I will face it just the same with God's love, His mercy, His grace and the power in His Word that has continuously given me strength when my spirit was weak." At the end of that thought I found myself in the middle of the parking lot. As my tears rested on my lower lashes I knew if one fell it would for sure drown me. It was one thing to make a choice to cut my hair, but to have no choice was a completely different story. So I called on Jesus to come and throw me a life preserver just to keep me from drowning in my own tears. Yes, at this point I was emotionally and physically drained after all of the surgeries and surgical procedures (three laparoscopies, an ovarian cyst removal, a dermoid tumor removed from the inside of an ovary along with half of the same ovary, two C-sections, three cystoscopies as well as three biopsies from my ovaries, uterus and bladder). At this point I knew for sure I couldn't handle any more on my own.

After dealing with the struggles of keeping normality in my day-to-day life I realized that many things would worsen my pain; stress, fear and worry were the components that would so often interrupt my relationship with God. So many times, when I couldn't shake my emotions, when I couldn't see beyond my fear and my mind was filled with things I couldn't control, I found myself existing through many dark days and many cold nights.

A Reflection of Hope

As time went on I remembered that I could have springtime in the winter. If I would just turn to God for all of my help, stay focused on His words of truth and remember who's in charge, I could be that one red rose blooming in the middle of a bed of white snow.

As my trials became plenty, each time I drew nearer to Christ.

> *Isaiah 43:2—When thou passest through the waters, I will be with thee; and through the rivers, they shall not overflow thee: when thou walkest through the fire, thou shalt not be burned; neither shall the flame kindle upon thee.*

never alone

Hello, Noel it's me.

There were many people in my life that disappeared because my life had become very painful for some to deal with. At first I felt sad because, when I cried out to many people to just listen, they had become deaf to the sound of my voice. I have reached for a friend to hold me up when I was falling, and that friend walked away, feeling that she couldn't help me. From my position I did not feel I was asking for much when I only needed an ear, or a shoulder, or just an encouraging word, but, in every circumstance, there is a lesson to be learned. I was seeking the wrong people for my comfort and understanding. Backs were turn on me because God was trying to get my attention. He was the only one that could help me. It gave my heart a new song to sing, a new beat to my drum and another opportunity for me to experience God's mercy and grace. Many people planned days and weeks at a time; I just prayed to get through the next moment without experiencing pain. Over time I had become more grateful, just enjoying the small things in life and so grateful to have a friend who would never leave me—my Lord Jesus Christ.

> *Proverbs 18:24—A man that hath friends must shew himself friendly: and there is a friend that sticketh closer than a brother.*

PART SIX

Reflection of Hope
(Dreams)

For this thing I besought the Lord thrice, that it might depart from me. And he said unto me, My grace is sufficient for thee: for my strength is made perfect in weakness. Most gladly therefore will I rather glory in my infirmities, that the power of Christ may rest upon me. Therefore I take pleasure in infirmities, in reproaches, in necessities, in persecutions, in distresses for Christ's sake: for when I am weak, then am I strong.

2 CORINTHIANS 12:8-10

mercy and grace

Hello, Noel it's me.

I sat on the side of my bed and the tears began to flow; I felt so alone in this invisible disorder, I felt as if no one knew my pain. I didn't know how to separate my illness as everyone else thought I should. The reality of what I felt day to day affected my life. I was so limited in what I could physically do. All my emotions had set in, my children always on my mind. I felt so bad with them having to continuously see me in a state of pain. I didn't want to frighten them when I screamed out in pain or scare them at just the sight of me not being able to get out of bed without help. I couldn't imagine what their little minds were processing, but I prayed continuously for God to manage their minds and to give me the comforting words to say to them.

I remember many days not being able to be around people, hearing my co-workers' and clients' voices, admiring many personalities and learning from so many testimonies. Although these things were missed due to my inability to work and my confinement to my home, I was blessed with a sound mind in which the memories of things missed were still there.

Huddled in my bed, enduring much pain, I found myself being swallowed up by fear of the unknown yet still reaching, grasping for hope and praying that God would wrap His arms around me and give me the strength I needed to endure and get through this trail just like many others. Never questioning why but always thinking in my mind, "Why not me? If it wasn't this it would be something else because you see we all must go through something."

The pain I speak of is called fibromyalgia, a musculoskeletal disorder.

> *Romans 5:1-2—Therefore being justified by faith, we have peace with God through our Lord Jesus Christ: By whom also we have access by faith into this grace wherein we stand, and rejoice in hope of the glory of God.*

pathway angels

Hello, Noel it's me.

It was amazing how God moved certain people out of my life and placed people in my life to aid me and my family in difficult times. The outpouring of concern, love and generosity came from many different paths that I had traveled. These people I called my pathway angels. We received phone calls from loved ones, prepared meals for weeks at a time, encouraging cards, some people would come and clean and do laundry, and I even had a girlfriend who would come bring me lunch and stay and visit during her lunch break. Others would come and take the children on fun outings or just entertain them while I rested. And the most important thing I knew was going on was prayer because each day my strength became stronger, I felt my spirit healing from the inside out, my heart and mind released the worry and I found joy and peace through my Lord, Jesus Christ. Noel, throughout the years I cried out to God in all my circumstances and every time He heard my cry and rescued me.

> *Psalm 62:8—Trust in him at all times;*
> *ye people, pour out your heart before him:*
> *God is a refuge for us. Selah.*

Part Seven

Reflection of Hope

*To every thing there is a season,
and a time to every purpose under the heaven.*

Ecclesiastes 3:1

the window

The evening before Noel was going to leave, she went to visit the window. As she kneeled she heard her name being called: "Noel, Noel, I knew you would come." Noel looked inside the window and she saw no one. She said, "Who are you and why has my whole vacation been filled with mysterious wonder? What is all this about? Am I loosing my mind or am I really stuck in a dream and yet to wake up?" Noel went on to say, "I am afraid of this feeling that I have within me; it is like no other feeling I have had before. It's as if my life is going to change and, for once, I don't know if I will be able to accept or control what happens to me."

The voice of the lady at the altar went on to say, "It was not a coincidence that your friends couldn't make it. It wasn't a coincidence that you were led to the window, and it is not a coincidence that, at this moment, you feel fear of the unknown. You see, it's all about God's divine plan, and from this moment on, your future will be all about the choices that you will make, not choices of whether you will turn right or left, but the choice of acceptances and realizing who's in control of your life. Noel, when I reveal myself to you, you will be very surprised; the outer appearance may be of a stranger, but I am a person whom you hold dear. Come visit me at the window before you leave tomorrow, and I'll explain everything to you."

On the last day of Noel's vacation it was if she had had a revelation. Noel found herself praying and having conversations with God in ways she had never experienced before. Taking sight of the mysterious woman's life had humbled Noel's spirit and opened her heart to receive a greater appreciation of life. She realized that her life wasn't all that bad, but, at any time, in a blink of an eye or many years of not really knowing what's important, a life could be changed. Noel dressed and headed to the window.

When she reached the window she stood with her hands gripping the sides of its pane, pressing her forehead on the glass with her eyes closed. A warm feeling came over her, calming her fears and nervousness.

Noel waited patiently for the mysterious woman and soon she heard a faint voice calling, "Noel, Noel."

Noel opened her eyes and replied, "I am here as you told me to be. Who are you and why have you consumed my thoughts, my dreams and my soul?"

"Before I reveal myself to you, you must hear what I have to say." Noel kneeled down on her knees and listened very intently. "Noel, I once tried to escape the pressures in my life with work and success; I tried to be all that others thought I should be, thinking I had control over my life, not needing any help from anyone but always trying to help others, thinking that all my strength came from a stalk of broccoli, liver once a week and a daily glass of milk. I never stopped to appreciate where I was in life and how I got there. My vision was success and living for the future, not taking time to thank God for just today. But, right in the midst of myself, God had other plans for me which headed me in a different direction—a path that I could not have traveled without Him, a path of humbleness, remembrance, strength, courage, endurance, love, peace and, most importantly, faith. Through all of my trials it was not for me to forget but to remember, to open my heart and acknowledge that God was in it. It was for me to look to the heavens and be showered with God's love. It was for me to realize that all my help comes from the Lord. Noel, still after all these years have gone by and one testimony has turned into many, I still find myself sitting by my window of hope. But instead of many tears of sorrow, I have many tears of joy because God has kept me on the path which He placed before me, and I endured and pressed on to do what He would have me do—be a reflection of hope to you. Even though my physical pain remains I sit patiently waiting, knowing what my God has already done. Noel, as you are headed back home you will only vaguely remember your dreams, and for me, well, I'll always be there, and, over time, you will see me and know me."

Tears began to flow from Noel's eyes. She cried out again, "Who are you and why have you consumed my thoughts, my dreams and my soul?"

"Noel, it is not about who I am, it is about who you are. I will reveal myself to you in time. But, whatever you do in your days to come, don't try to detour but remember that, on this vacation, you opened your heart and realized that God was in it. Noel, I must go now, and surely I will see you very soon."

The Window

Noel wiped her tears and began walking slowly up the beach. When she reached the beach house, she gathered her things and headed to the airport.

the beginning

Noel had a great flight, and when she returned home, her life went on as usual. She was still busy, busy, busy working even harder for a promotion on her job. As an event planner and decorator, taking care of her clients was what she lived for, never stopping to take a break. Noel couldn't remember her dreams nor could she remember the lady, but she had began to feel as if someone was always in her presence.

Noel begin to pray more often, and, instead of working on Sundays, she began to attend Sunday morning worship. But, one day while in a marketing meeting presenting a floor plan for 1200 guests in the hotel ballroom for New Years' Eve, Noel fell to the floor in excruciating pain. She was rushed to the hospital and into surgery right away. As Noel lay on the operating table surrounded by white walls her head was turned to one side and a white sheet covered her body from her feet to midway up her chest. Noel's body shivered from the cold air that blew throughout the room. From the way she lay on the operating table, focused and humble, she seemed to have no

The Window

fear, but surely Noel was afraid. Suddenly, she began to speak aloud, "Lord, God, don't let this slow me down because I'm still in search of that road that will lead me into the rest of my life. Guide the hands of the surgeons and I'll talk with you when you awake me."

The surgical team entered the room all suited up in their blue attire, little caps that covered most of their heads and masks that covered their noses and mouths leaving only their eyes showing. There was much conversation going on in preparation for the surgery as the anesthesiologist began to inject the anesthesia into Noel's IV.

Noel's eyes closed and an oxygen mask was placed over her mouth and nose. She began drifting off in minutes, but just before she was totally unconscious, Noel heard a familiar voice calling her name. "Noel, Noel, it's me, the lady at the altar." Noel opened her eyes and the doors of the operating room opened and the lady extended her hand and led Noel to the window. As they walked along the beach toward the window, the beach seemed to have taken on a different atmosphere. There wasn't a person in sight; the surroundings had become very tranquil. The water was still and it seemed to watch them as they moved slowly across the crystal-like sand. The skies were blue and the church seemed to pull them closer and closer. When Noel reached the window, she realized that the lady was no longer with her. Noel cried out as she fell to her knees gripping the side of the window pane as a warm feeling came over her, calming her fears and nervousness, "Who are you?"

Noel waited patiently to hear from the lady and suddenly the lady spoke, "Noel if you will remember the last day of your vacation, I told you that it was not about who I was but about who you are." Tears began to roll from Noel's eyes as she

A Reflection of Hope

pressed her forehead against the window. When she looked inside bits and pieces of her dreams were flashed before her eyes. Noel couldn't believe what she was seeing, and suddenly all of the lights in the church went out. Noel then said, "My dreams and the lady in them... could that have been me?"

"Noel, in your days to come don't try to detour but endure and press on. God will always be with you. Now, Noel, the doors of the church are open. Please come and take your place."

Noel raised to her feet and walked to the church doors and there was a burst of light shining that made her hesitate. When the light was lifted the church was no longer a church but an operating room. The lady called to Noel and said, "Take my hand and come with me."

As Noel began to walk closer to the operating table the lady said, "I told you in time you would see me and know me. Come, Noel, and take your place in your life."

When Noel reached the operating table, the lady turned her head and Noel saw herself. She then reached out and touched her own face and climbed upon the operating table and began to weep. There stood a lady on the outside looking in the window, and the lady's tears were in sync with Noel's tears. Then Noel heard a voice from Heaven saying, "Noel, I am with you now and I will always be with you. I'll be with you at that road that leads you into the rest of your life. The road is here and the beginning is now. Let your life be a reflection of hope to others looking on."

A cyst the size of a grapefruit was then removed from Noel's right ovary.

The Window

Romans 15:13—Now the God of hope fill you with all joy and peace in believing, that ye may abound in hope, through the power of the Holy Ghost.

In everything give God thanks!

Psalm 119:111—Thy testimonies have I taken as an heritage for ever: for they are the rejoicing of my heart.

Psalm 34:4—I sought the LORD, and he heard me, and delivered me from all my fears.

Psalm 61:1-2—Hear my cry, O God: attend unto my prayer. From the end of the earth will I cry unto thee, when my heart is overwhelmed: lead me to the rock that is higher than I.

1 Corinthians 13:7—Beareth all things, believeth all things, hopeth all things, endureth all things.

Psalm 119:49-50—Remember the word unto thy servant upon which thou hast caused me to hope. This is my comfort in my affliction: for thy word hath quickened me.

Psalm 119:71—It is good for me that I have been afflicted; that I might learn thy statutes.

A Reflection of Hope

2 Corinthians 1:3-4—Praise be to the God and Father of our Lord Jesus Christ, the Father of compassion and the God of all comfort, who comforts us in all our troubles, so that we can comfort those in any trouble with the comfort we ourselves have received from God (NIV).

To the many reflections of life, thank you for visiting my window of hope and engulfing many pages of God's love, mercy and grace. In all my challenges and afflictions God has allowed me to have a new vision beyond sight, meaning that I can see beyond my situations because, in my window, the reflection is of Christ. I encourage you today to stop right in the middle of your situation and acknowledge that God is always available.

For those of you who think God is out of reach, just reach and he will grab you.

For those who are falling, God will catch you.

For those of you who feel that you can't walk your path alone, God will be with you.

For those who are in the middle of affliction, God can heal you, from the inside out.

The Window

Let every life be a window which brings forth a reflection of the manifestation of Christ that reveals a ray of light and hope one to another.

Oh Spirit

As i call upon You with the invitation
to invade the very essence of my existence,
i humble my heart and yield to the things
that are not of You.

My heart is a sponge, yearning to absorb
the overflowing love that You have for me.

Oh Spirit…

Place me in your care,
for the circumstances that i face,
i shall not even dare.

Uplift my stance, so i may stand and praise the Son,
the One who gave me life, joy and victory in pain.

Oh Spirit…

As i kneel beneath the heavens,
send the rain and wash away the stains,

unfold the sun from the clouds
and dry the tears from my weeping eyes,
place the moon to give light
to the darkness of my path.

Oh Spirit…

As i call upon You, embed Your presence within me,
for i now know that it is You that has come to set me free.

Oh Spirit…

How grateful i am to Thee.

~Olga J. Walker

book reviews

In a straight forward way, like the apostle Paul who heard the Lord say to him, "My grace is sufficient for you, for power is made perfect in weakness," the author, Olga J. Walker, has arrived at such a point where she can use some of her life's thorns to inspire courage and patience in other sufferers.

Rev. Myron F. McCoy
St. Mark U.M.C.
Chicago, IL

The level of wellness one experiences can be measured in many ways. However the pathway to receiving total wellness is through faith in God. I encourage others to engage in reading The Window: A Reflection of Hope, *as you will see how faith in God encourages the heart to overcome life's unforeseen circumstances.*

Reginald Spight, Pastor
Living Water Church
Memphis, TN